P9-DEH-006

WORDBIRDS

*An Irreverent Lexicon
for the 21st Century*

By LIESL SCHILLINGER

ILLUSTRATIONS BY

ELIZABETH ZECHEL

SIMON & SCHUSTER

New York   London   Toronto   Sydney   New Delhi

3 1357 00305 8796

Simon & Schuster
1230 Avenue of the Americas
New York, NY 10020

Copyright © 2013 by Liesl Schillinger and Elizabeth Zechel

All rights reserved, including the right to reproduce this book or portions thereof
in any form whatsoever. For information address Simon & Schuster Subsidiary
Rights Department, 1230 Avenue of the Americas, New York, NY 10020.

First Simon & Schuster hardcover edition October 2013

SIMON & SCHUSTER and colophon are registered trademarks of
Simon & Schuster, Inc.

For information about special discounts for bulk purchases,
please contact Simon & Schuster Special Sales at 1-866-506-1949
or business@simonandschuster.com.

The Simon & Schuster Speakers Bureau can bring authors to your live event.
For more information or to book an event contact the Simon & Schuster Speakers
Bureau at 1-866-248-3049 or visit our website at www.simonspeakers.com.

DESIGNED BY ERICH HOBBING

Manufactured in the United States of America

1   3   5   7   9   10   8   6   4   2

Library of Congress Cataloging-in-Publication Data

Schillinger, Liesl.
Wordbirds : an irreverent lexicon for the 21st century / by Liesl Schillinger ;
illustrations by Elizabeth Zechel. — First Simon & Schuster hardcover edition.
p. cm
1. English language—New words. I. Zechel, Elizabeth, illustrator. II. Title.
PE1583.S35 2013
422—dc23
2013008365

ISBN 978-1-4767-1348-9
ISBN 978-1-4767-1350-2(ebook)

To my mother and father,
с любовью

WORDBIRD

Wordbird (**n.**) *'wurd-burd* A memorable neologism whose meaning can be effectively and whimsically enhanced by an accompanying bird drawing.

> *"I wish there was a word for the relief I felt when I skipped Pat's awards dinner," said Daisy.*
> *"Actually, there IS a word for that," said Ian. "It's a wordbird, 'CANCELLELATION'—and it's illustrated by a grinning Snowy Owl."*

AUTHOR'S NOTE

Historically, lexicographers—that is, the scholars and logophiles who write dictionaries—have been cautious, prudent types. For centuries they've moved at a glacial pace, ponderously deliberating the worth of new words, and skeptically scrutinizing usage examples. Very occasionally, and almost grudgingly, they have concluded that a neologism deserves a spot on the permanent record, and have nudged it into the lexicon with a sigh of erudite resignation. Such conscientiousness is admirable. But over the last two decades, new technologies, new means of communication, and sweeping social changes have crashed down on society like an avalanche. The old dictionary has not expanded quickly enough to keep up with the ever-evolving backdrop of daily life in the twenty-first century. The coinages you will find in *Wordbirds* address this lapse, providing new language that puts the way we live now into words—accompanied by illustrations of more than a hundred and fifty singularly expressive actual birds, on the logic that, as the sixties rock band the Trashmen put it: "The bird is the word."

WORDBIRDS

I.

Fashion and Style

The twenty-first century is an intensely visual age, in which, thanks to an ever blurrier definition of gender, an ever sharper definition of physical perfection, and an ever more indulgent attitude toward cosmetic self-enhancement, more and more people choose to look exactly as they wish, without fear of becoming laughingstocks. (Or rather, without fear that anyone will have the guff to let them know they have become laughingstocks.)

ANOREXUAL

Anorexual (**n.**) *an-nur-'rek-shoo-al* One who equates emaciation with intellectual rigor, and despises people whose bodies do not reflect that value. Also (**adj.**)

Dale looked skeptically at the man he was interviewing for the museum internship. Sure, the guy's résumé was strong, but he was plump—unlike anorexual Dale, who was skeletally lean. Could such a puffy person 'get' Giacometti? Dale doubted it.

APLORABLE

Aplorable (**adj.**) *a-'plor-a-bul* Descriptive term for roly-poly creatures that are both incredibly cute and somewhat grotesque, like shar-peis.

Strangers oohed and aahed over Ada and Ludo, but their father secretly thought his children's creased, pudgy, Yoda-like faces made them look more aplorable than adorable.

BAITFACE

Baitface (**n.**) *'bayt-fayss* Sociophobe whose mouth, nostrils, eyebrows, etc. are abundantly pierced with metal rings, studs, and gewgaws.

The teenage baitfaces who hung out around Astor Place gave Miranda the willies. She thought all the hoops and pins dangling from their lips made them look like battle-scarred trout.

BRIGHTBITE

Brightbite (**n.**) *'bryt-byt* One who bleaches his teeth until they reach an implausible degree of whiteness.

Ick, a brightbite, Samantha thought, as she smiled with false enthusiasm at her blind date, whose teeth had been whitened until they looked like plastic piano keys.

CHROMAZONE

Chromazone **(n.)** *'kro-ma-zone* The eerie phenomenon whereby an inexplicably high number of people turn out to have chosen to dress in the identical color on the same day—like puce, aqua, or lime green.

> *"Look!—we're in the chromazone," Robert crowed as he walked into his office in saffron-yellow jeans. Lakshmi was wearing a dress of the exact same shade, and Darrel harmonized in a mango-colored sweater.*

COUNTERCOOLTURE

Countercoolture **(n.)** *'kown-ter-kool-cher* The unhurried, cooler-than-thou hipster clerks who work at juice bars, bookstores, bubble tea parlors, and vintage boutiques. Also the mood they collectively project.

> *"Quit scowling," Lance whispered to Hank. "If the countercoolture picks up on your impatience, we'll never get our lattes."*

EXESHOETION

Exeshoetion (n.) *ek-suh-'shu-shun* The destruction of a fine pair of shoes (usually accidental).

After the rain stopped, Rowan put on his Gommino loafers and went out to walk the dog. When Amos lunged at a squirrel, Rowan was pulled into a puddle, causing the exeshoetion of his brand-new shoes.

HYPERSCENTILATE

Hyperscentilate **(v.)** *hy-per-'sent-a-layt* To apply too much perfume, surrounding yourself in a thick, aromatic mist that causes people to choke, sneeze, and cough.

As soon as Neil stepped into the elevator, he started wheezing, his asthma set off by the cloying cloud of Flowerbomb somebody had hyperscentilated.

MASCULARA

Masculara **(n.)** *mas-kew-'lair-a* Mascara, when applied by trendy men.

Ryan glued on fake eyelashes, then brushed them thickly with masculara to achieve the desired wicked raptor look.

MOOD HAIR

Mood hair (**n. phrase**) *'mood hehr* A phenomenon associated with those whose hair color starts the month in vivid hue, but fades over the weeks to a pale shadow . . . only to return to vibrancy when a new box of dye is deployed.

> *The TV anchor's mood hair typically fluctuated between lemon-yellow and cotton-white, but on rare occasions it would glow orange, or even green.*

NOSEBLOB

Noseblob (**n.**) *'noaz-blob* The result of an overly thorough nose job, which leaves the patient with too little trace of his formerly distinguishing feature.

Monica asked the surgeon to make her nose look like Kate Middleton's, but the resulting noseblob made her look more like a Muppet than a princess.

PARROT-TOPS

Parrot-tops (**n. pl.**) *'pehr-ruht-'tops* Fashion victims who dye their hair in vivid or pastel shades—making it look from a distance as if tropical birds were roosting on their shoulders. (Also refers to the hairstyle itself.)

> *So many parrot-tops crowded the dance floor at Mighty that the place looked like a whirling kaleidoscope as strobe lights bounced off all the multicolored heads.*

SANDACLES

Sandacles **(n.)** *'san-da-kulz* Trendy sandals encumbered with gladiator-style cuffs and straps, chains, fringe, and other trinketry.

Freya was enormously proud of her $600 feathered sandacles, and didn't mind that they clanked when she walked.

SEPHORAID

Sephoraid (**n.**) *suh-'for-ayd* A stealthy invasion of a Sephora store made on the way to a date or a party, in which you use the store's makeup and perfume then leave without buying anything. Also (**v.**) and (**ger.**) **Sephoraiding**

> *Catching her reflection in a window, Gwen saw that her makeup had worn off, so she ducked into a shop and did a Sephoraid to spruce up on her way to meet Jake at the movies.*

SHIGHTS

Shights (**n.**) *shytz* Inane fashion trend of wearing shorts over tights or patterned leggings.

The L train was filled with sloe-eyed young women in shights and wedge-heeled espadrilles, who reminded Seth somehow of a parody of Swan Lake, *with dancers in shorts instead of tutus.*

SHOEICIDE

Shoeicide (**n.**) *'shoo-iss-syd* The act of destroying your feet by deliberately wearing shoes you suspect or know to be excruciatingly painful, usually out of vanity.

Letitia willfully committed shoeicide at the big party, wearing a pair of five-inch designer heels that made her toes go numb. Within half an hour, she couldn't stand, much less dance.

SHUTTERSTRUTTER

Shutterstrutter **(n.)** *'shut-tur-'strut-tur* An aspiring or (more rarely) professional photographer who strolls through public places sporting a high-end camera, hoping to attract admiring attention.

As Robin sat at the café table, a shutterstrutter passed by, then paused and doubled back. Conspicuously focusing his Leica, he snapped a dozen shots, then gave Robin a smoldering glance, flicked his long black hair, and sauntered off.

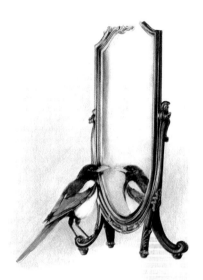

SOLOOKSIST

Solooksist **(n.)** *'sol-look-sist* Vain person who never passes up an opportunity to admire himself or herself in any reflective surface.

Walking through the mall with Trevor took ages because he was such a solooksist, and slowed in front of every shop window to preen.

SUISTYLE

Suistyle (**v. or n.**) *'soo-iss-styl* To get (or to give yourself) a hideously unflattering haircut or hairdo; also the resulting coiffure.

After her horrible breakup, Pamela impetuously took a pair of scissors to her long hair, wanting to give herself a new look. The resulting suistyle made her resemble Moe from the Three Stooges.

YOUTHFLAKE

Youthflake (**n.**) *'yooth-flayk* Adult who mimics the dress style of the younger generation, or who continues to dress as if he or she were still in his or her teens or twenties.

The Grateful Dead tribute concert was packed with crinkly youthflakes, decked out in faded tie-dye from the 1970s.

II.

Politics, Media, and Celebrity

Never before have so many people had so much access to the private and public thoughts and actions of people they don't know—from politicians, protesters, journalists, and movie stars to publicity seekers and YouTube heroes at home and abroad. The curious public, abetted by news spinners on cable TV, radio, and the Web, make sure that no awkward remark goes unreported and that every outrageous statement or photograph goes viral. Somewhere along the line, marketers have decided this state of affairs is desirable, and instructed authors and newsmakers to blog and tweet so as to draw as many fans as possible. Even Nobelists, presidents, and popes have to have Twitter handles . . . if they hope to stay relevant to, you know . . . whoever.

ACTORVIST

Actorvist (**n.**) *'ak-tur-vist* A star who uses celebrity as a soap-box for political punditry—for good or ill.

While Ben Affleck unleashed his actorvism on the Congo, and Leonardo DiCaprio used his to spread awareness of global warming, the actorvist Ashley Judd mulled a Senate run in Kentucky.

BLOGGERDUDGEON

Bloggerdudgeon **(n.)** *'blog-gur-'dudj-jun* The sense of indignation, injury, and self-pity felt by gossip bloggers when they themselves receive unflattering attention.

Natasha enjoyed mocking the great and sort-of-great on her snarky blog, and her posts had helped destroy several budding careers. But when a journalist attacked her on a radio show, she posted a battery of angry self-justifications dripping with bloggerdudgeon.

CELEBUTAUNT

Celebutaunt (**v.**) *suh-'leb-yu-tawnt* To gloat over the flaws, misfortunes, or gaffes of celebrities. Also (**n.**) a published item or spoken remark that mocks a celeb.

Evan was obsessed with reality TV, and loved to come up with stinging put-downs of cast members to make his friends laugh. But when he launched a blog to spread his celebutaunts, it went viral, and he became a target of celebutaunting himself.

CONSERVASCHISM

Conservaschism **(n.)** *kun-'sur-va-'skiz-um* The early-twenty-first-century political divide in the U.S. Congress between moderate Republicans and far-right extremists who refuse compromise at any cost.

> *Because of the conservaschism, one Republican senator opposed immigration reforms he had once championed and another filibustered his own bill in an effort to court hardliners in the party.*

CONTAMINOTION

Contaminotion (**n.**) *kun-tam-i-'no-shun* A spurious, wrong-headed idea that spreads virally and poisons public discourse.

Was it true that the uterus possessed the power to stave off unwanted pregnancies; that global warming was a myth; and that most Americans thought they should have the right to own assault weapons? No, but such contaminotions poured daily into the ears of millions of commuters as they listened to hate radio.

DEMONSTAYTION

Demonstaytion (**n.**) *dem-mun-'stay-shun* A political protest that gathers strength when its participants remain on a particular site over time.

Inspired by the protesters in Tahrir Square in Cairo, the Occupy Wall Street protesters staged demonstaytions for months, refusing to leave the city plazas where they had set up camp, though they made no explicit demands.

DOPPELGAZER

Doppelgazer (n.) *'dop-pul-gay-zur* Starstruck person who's constantly convincing himself he's spotted a celeb, only to realize as the V.I.P. draws near that it's an ordinary person after all. Also (v.) doppelgaze

Stephanie doppelgazed as she cruised Ocean Drive in the rental car with Deanna, squealing every other minute that she had sighted a movie star or celebrity chef; but on closer inspection, it always turned out to be just another tourist.

JOURNALEER

Journaleer (**n.**) *'jur-na-'leer* Commentator on news programs, blogs, and opinion pages who vigorously holds forth on the topics of the day, whether or not he is informed on the issues. Also (**v.**)

Josh never read books, newspapers, or magazines; he got all of his information by watching self-anointed experts journaleer about the headlines on talk shows.

LADYFLACKER

Ladyflacker **(n.)** *'lay-dee-flak-kur* Female nonfiction writer who writes predominantly about her own sexual exploits and/or gynecological concerns, and on woman-centered gender issues. Also **(ger.)** **Ladyflacking**

> *"Did you read that book* Marry Him!*—about how women should settle for someone they don't love if they don't want to die alone?"*
>
> *"Alas, no. But I subscribe to* The Atlantic, *so I caught the gist back when it was just a ladyflacker essay."*

PINK'D

Pink'd (v.) *pinkt* To be falsely branded a communist, leftie, or socialist by right-wing political activists. (In the spirit of Ashton Kutcher's *Punk'd*, but less lighthearted.)

> *When President Obama bailed out General Motors, Rush Limbaugh pink'd him, denouncing his "socialist" agenda.*

TELAVERSION

Telaversion **(n.)** *'tel-a-vur-zhun* A publicly proclaimed hatred of (and ignorance of) television. Often a pose. Also **(adj.) Telaverse**

Olivia told anyone who would listen that she was telaverse, had never seen a reality TV show, and didn't even own a television. She swore her favorite diversion was reading the New York Review of Books. *Secretly, though, she watched* The Bachelor *on Hulu at home on her laptop.*

TELETHARGY

Telethargy (**n.**) *tel-'leth-er-jee* Highly contagious feeling of lassitude and crankiness resulting from (for instance) watching too much *Antiques Road Show*, C-SPAN, or similar.

On a snowy Sunday in February, Cliff and Brent meant to go out for brunch and maybe check out the flea markets. Instead they succumbed to telethargy for hours, watching terrible television shows until they got headaches.

TWEET SHOW

Tweet show (**n.**) *'tweet sho* Salacious nude or suggestive photos sent out on the Internet via Twitter.

"Do you remember that tweet show Anthony Weiner sent out? All those photos of himself in his underwear?"

"No, I've been blindfolded, under a rock, wearing earplugs for years. What are you talking about?"

TWITLER

Twitler **(n.)** *'twit-lur* Vociferous person who uses Twitter to bully others, particularly public figures.

After twenty twitlers flamed his seven p.m. broadcast, Lyle changed the lineup of his nine p.m. show, hoping to win friendlier comments from the blogosphere.

III.

Friends, Frenemies, and Fellow Students

Who or what is it that sucks up the bulk of your attention when you're supposed to be studying, making home improvements, or prudently readying yourself to tackle the new century? Is it John Maynard Keynes? Faux-malachiting? Urban rebounding? Online personality tests? Or could it be, rather, the largish group of people with whom you spend hours talking each day, in person or on-screen—the people you see in class or in the corridor, and whom you meet for lunch or dinner, go to games, movies, and the beach with, and incessantly compare yourself to? That's right, it's your *friends*—those indispensable, ever-changing legions of contemporaries who are so much more entertaining than your parents, yet whose phone numbers you don't know by heart. Not to worry, their digits are safe in your cell phone address book . . . that is, until your frenemy spills Coke on your phone, or a rogue houseguest steals it.

BAD FAIRY

Bad Fairy (**n. phrase**) *'bad 'fehr-ee* Like the malicious god-mother who cursed the infant Sleeping Beauty, a Bad Fairy unnerves you by barraging you with dark judgments when you seek her support.

When Todd called his friend Matt for consolation after Lauren dumped him, Matt went Bad Fairy on him—pointing out that all his relationships failed, and that he was way too old for Lauren anyway—even though, he added, she was not good enough for him.

DOOMMATE

Doommate (**n.**) *'doom-mayt* A roommate whom you tolerate by necessity, but who is difficult, even dangerous, to live with.

The sublet was only $300 a month, but it came with a doommate who drank too much tequila, smoked menthols, and was prone to night rages. Chris signed the lease all the same—an unpaid intern could not afford to be picky.

DUMPSTER DÉCOR

Dumpster décor (**n. phrase**) *'dum-stur duh-'kor* Unlovely cast-off furniture scavenged by impecunious or trendily ascetic types to furnish their abodes.

Keith and Ben were proud of the ripped sofabed and sagging armchair they'd pulled from the street for their dorm, but when their parents visited during Family Weekend, they were so appalled by the dumpster décor that they rushed to Target to buy them a cheap living room suite and a can of bedbug spray.

FREUDSCHADE

Freudschade (**n.**) '*froyd-shah-duh* Annoyance at being used continually as a therapist by friends or relatives who have no interest in any conversation that does not directly involve their own issues.

Michael hadn't seen Lana in a year; so when he got back from Iraq, he agreed to have a drink and "catch up." But for two hours, she'd talked nonstop about her boyfriend and her boss, which left Michael overflowing with freudschade, and almost wishing he was back in Baghdad.

GLOSS POSSE

Gloss posse (**n.**) *'gloss-'poss-see* Group of (usually) teenage girls obsessed with their appearance, who at all times are engaged in applying makeup and brushing and flipping their hair.

> *"Is that the debate team?"*
>
> *"You mean those girls by the lockers, smearing Juicy Tubes on their lips? No, that's a gloss posse."*

HOMEBUDDY

Homebuddy (n.) *'hoam-bud-dee* Friend who always wants to socialize by having people come to his or her place.

Cal's friends didn't mind trekking to his loft for Magic Hat and poker—his eternal standing offer. They knew he was a homebuddy. But on the Fourth of July, they wanted to watch fireworks at a roof party barbecue, not play cards in Cal's kitchen.

IDOLOATHE

Idoloathe (v.) *'eye-duh-lothe* To bear feelings of admiration mingled with envy and hatred for a gifted, successful, lucky, and/or attractive person whose excellence makes you feel pathetic in comparison.

> *Yeah, she's gorgeous—so much fun, and only twenty-four! I can't believe she got into the Whitney Biennial. I kind of idoloathe her.*

INVIPAYTION

Invipaytion **(n.)** *in-vih-'pay-shun* An invitation to something marvelous—like a destination wedding, a St. Moritz ski trip, an African safari, or an exclusive club—that, if accepted, will incur extraordinary expense.

Taylor and Joel were overjoyed that so many of their friends could now legally wed. But after accepting five invipaytions, they balked at the expense of buying so many plane tickets and extravagant presents, and backed out of two of them.

RECOGNORE

Recognore (v.) 'rek-ig-'nor To pretend not to see someone
you know when it might be awkward to say hello.

Bruce saw Carolyn jogging by the river but recognored
her, figuring she wouldn't appreciate being stopped mid-
run.

ROONEY

Rooney **(n.)** *'roo-nee* One who, like the late Andy Rooney of *60 Minutes,* always has something to say, seeks the last word, and enjoys posing rhetorical questions like "D'ja ever wonder?"

"Margaret, you're being a rooney, knock it off," Lisa whispered, as her teammate paused for breath, poised to regale their table with yet another story of her heroics on the soccer field.

RSVTEASE

RSVTease (**n.**) *ar-ess-vee-'teez* Desired guest who habitually responds to invitations by saying he will come, but who never (or hardly ever) makes an appearance.

> *Tristan said he was coming to the party but Marisol didn't bother to set a place at the table for him, because he was such a well-known RSVTease.*

SHAREMONGER

Sharemonger (**n.**) *'shayr-mon-gur* Person who rallies a group to join a house share at the beach, on a lake, or in the country-side, then must hound his friends to pay their part of the rent while wrangling with the property owner and juggling house members' changing weekend requests.

"I want to spend three weeks on Fire Island this summer, but I don't want to be the sharemonger—it's too much work! Do you know anyone who's got a place we can glom on to?"

SHOWPSHAW

Showpshaw (**n.**) *'shope-shaw* A person "puts on a showp-shaw" when he deflects a compliment by denying it was justified.

When the guys at the pickup basketball game thumped Pete on the back for acing the free throw, Pete protested, "It was just luck!" But nobody bought his showpshaw.

SLUSHEEFUND

Slusheefund **(n.)** *'sluh-shee-fund* Parentally supplied gas card or "emergency" credit card, used by a young person to charge Doritos, Slurpees, condoms, candy bars, and sundries at Quik Marts and student unions for herself and anyone in her entourage.

Carrie promised her parents she'd only use the credit card they gave her for school supplies and "emergencies," but by Christmas of freshman year, she'd chalked up $800 on the slusheefund on hot dogs, Häagen-Dazs, and Red Bull at Wawa . . . and seemingly become the most popular girl on her floor.

SOCIAL CRAWLER

Social crawler (**n.**) *'so-shul 'kraw-lur* One who mingles aspirationally with people he (wrongly) considers select. Also (**n.**) **Social crawling**

> *After attending beer-soaked networking events for a year, Arthur realized with self-loathing that the gatherings he'd chosen were Z-list, not A-list, and that he'd been social crawling ever since he'd moved to the city.*

IV.

The Office

In the age of "tribes" in which we find ourselves, millennials migrate from job to job, city to city, leaving hometowns and relatives far behind. The office becomes a kind of home, and friends and coworkers can substitute for family. This is lucky, as, often enough, everyone's parents and siblings have long since moved away too, and have busy careers of their own: home is a glimmer in the ether (even if most people find a real-world gathering point at Thanksgiving). In the workplace, the ties that arise between friends and colleagues can provide a reassuring sense of belonging, but have the nonfamilial advantage of being severable if they turn sour.

ALTER-EVIL

Alter-evil (**n.**) *'al-tur-'ee-vul* A colleague or other contemporary for whom you nurse a perverse antipathy because he resembles you in significant ways, fostering feelings of competition and self-loathing.

> *Henry bristled as Clay walked into the screening room with a coterie of his staffers. They'd gone to the same schools and ended up in the same business. How had his alter-evil come so far, so fast, when Henry was still struggling to make his name?*

CUBICLE QUEEN

Cubicle queen (**n.**) *'kyoo-bi-kul 'kween* One who overdresses and/or wears too much makeup at the office.

At the DMV, Ty handed his birth certificate and driver's license application to a cubicle queen with false eyelashes, who snatched the forms from him with startling, glitter-manicured hands.

E-QUAIL

E-quail (**v.**) *'ee-kwayl* To feel dread upon receiving an e-mail from a hostile or irksome source, and to resist opening it for fear it might contain distressing or irritating news, or increase your workload.

> *When a message from his boss landed in his inbox, Rowan e-quailed and scrolled down the screen so he wouldn't have to even look at it.*

FLOUNDER

Flounder **(n.)** *'flown-dur* A diffident, socially inept person who stares at the floor when conversing with others, avoiding eye contact.

Delia's heart sank as the new manager shook hands with her team, keeping his eyes riveted on the carpet throughout the introductions. Oh, terrific, a flounder, *she thought ironically.* That'll be great for morale.

FRATOIS

Fratois (n.) *'frat-twah* A hearty slang or patois used by bonhomous men that makes them sound like back-slapping fraternity brothers.

> *"Sweet!" Jeremy yelped as he saw Mark, one cubicle away, arc a wad of trash into a wastebasket.*
> *"Thanks, bro!" Mark responded.*
> *"You the man!" Jeremy replied, fist-bumping him.*
> *And Melanie sighed, tired of hearing her forty-year-old coworkers speak fratois.*

GULLIGAL

Gulligal **(n.)** *'gul-lig-gal* A canny woman who pretends to be naïve and unambitious in order to attract allies and disarm potential foes.

When Beryl started out at the TV show as an intern, she put herself down, flattered her coworkers, asked everyone for advice, and appeared unthreatening at all times. Within two years, the gulligal was promoted to co-anchor. She had not watched All About Eve *for nothing.*

HOLLOWGRAM

Hollowgram (**n.**) *'hawl-o-gram* An e-mail to which you forgot to attach a file before hitting Send.

"Oops, I sent you a hollowgram by mistake—here it is again, this time with *the attachment!"*

IMPEDIMENTOR

Impedimentor (n.) *im-'ped-i-'men-tor* A successful, accomplished older person who chooses not to instruct or assist young people who look up to him or her, intentionally thwarting their progress.

Deborah eagerly joined the team of a high-powered attorney she admired, not knowing her boss was an impedimentor who resented young associates, took credit for their work, and blamed them for his own mistakes.

MEGATASKING

Megatasking (**n.**) *'meh-ga-tass-king* Accomplishing an exceptionally large number of varied tasks in a short period of time (a very rare occurrence).

Kenneth woke up at six, jogged three miles, raked the yard, went to the office, and finished two projects. Back home after supper, he fixed the screen door, helped the boys with their homework, then stained the new shelf in the study. Were the krill oil pills Betsy had pushed on him responsible for his megatasking? He took two more, just in case.

MUMBLENYM

Mumblenym (**n.**) *'mum-bul-nim* Word you don't know how to pronounce, usually because you've seen it written but never heard it spoken, like "misled" or "awry."

Marc cringed when Karen told their hosts that the cabaret was "lowsh." He realized that "louche" was a mumblenym for her—she'd only seen it in writing, so she didn't know it was pronounced "loosh."

MUTE POINT

Mute point (**n. phrase**) *myoot-'poynt* When somebody in a group makes a good suggestion, but somehow, nobody hears it.

At the planning meeting, Marisol proposed a terrific idea for cost-cutting. As usual, nobody paid attention, but ten minutes later, Elliott co-opted her mute point and got credit for it.

NETSHIRKING

Netshirking (**n.**) *'net-shur-king* Falling behind in work because you have attended too many work-related social events in a row, and (typically) downed too many free, unwanted drinks, resulting in groggy mornings-after. Also (**v.**) **Netshirk**

"How's the hybrid design going?"

"Actually, I'm a little behind. Last week was the auto show, and what with all the netshirking, I kind of lost momentum."

OCCUPLAYTION

Occuplaytion (**n.**) *ock-yoo-'play-shun* A non-demanding, non-threatening, fanciful "job" invented for heroines of Hollywood romantic comedies.

> *Mindy used to want to be a plant waterer like Drew Barrymore in* Music and Lyrics; *or a corporate gifter like Marilu Henner in* L.A. Story; *or a village chocolatier like Juliette Binoche in* Chocolat. *But when she was eighteen, she realized there were no real jobs like those occuplaytions in Little Rock, so she got a job at Avis.*

SCREENRAVER

Screenraver (**n.**) *'skreen-ray-vur* A colleague who talks back to his or her computer all day long, responding to such stimuli as news items, e-mail, videos, photos, etc. Also (**v.**) **Screenrave** and (**ger.**) **Screenraving**

Nandi was trying to file her report, but the World Cup finals were on, and the cheers and shouts from the screenravers watching the game in the cubicles around hers made it impossible to concentrate.

SUPERPERVISOR

Superpervisor (n.) *soo-per-'purv-vyz-ur* Supervisor known for making hiring choices based on sex appeal, and/or for making inappropriate overtures to employees.

On her first day of work Jessica thought it was odd that so many women in her department looked like her—petite and red-haired. But when the boss came over and started flirting, she realized it was no accident; he was a superpervisor, and she was his "type."

WORDPECKER

Wordpecker (**n.**) *'wurd-pek-ker* Someone who types so loudly, emphatically, and resoundingly that nobody nearby can hold a thought.

As Christine sat at her desk in the newsroom, attempting to conduct a phone interview with a congressman, the rat-a-tat-tapping from the wordpeckers around her made it impossible to hear anything the man was saying.

V.

The Way We Live Now

Harried and distracted by their unending workdays, and bewildered by the flood of audiovisual come-ons that rush at them from screens (even in elevators!), contemporary citizens can feel as if their minds were set on "whir." As jolts from the global economy and climate change send shudders down Main Street, the world feels smaller, busier, and more stressful every day. Plus, those who use social media (and who doesn't?) are prey to the niggling suspicion that they're missing out, and that the Joneses across the street—or the Patels, Wangs, and Shcherbatskys across the ocean—have more luck, fun, and free time than they do, if Pinterest is any proof. Although the maladies of the millennial mindset may not be exactly curable, there's satisfaction to be found in putting names to them. And perhaps, hashtags.

ANTICIHATION

Anticihation (**n.**) *an-tiss-i-'hay-shun* The emotion of brooding resentment felt by someone who has to do something he hates that's supposed to be a treat.

Charles stewed in anticihation before taking his wife to see Giselle *at the Met for her birthday. She loved ballet, but he would rather have gone to the dentist.*

APOCAPIC

Apocapic (**n.**) *a-ˈpok-a-pik* Any of the hundreds of bleak films portraying cataclysmic events, which draw fervent audiences of popcorn-crunching pessimists and environmentalists who believe the end of the world is nigh.

Annika and Liam wanted to see a feel-good movie, but all that was playing at the multiplex was a zombie flick and an apocapic about the 2004 tsunami.

APOLOGIBE

Apologibe (**v.**) *a-'pawl-a-dzhyb* To excuse oneself insincerely in a peevish manner that shows no regret is felt.

As Lloyd hunched over the best sellers table, his backpack blocking the aisle, a woman pushed past him, knocking his backpack to the ground. "I'm so sorry for intruding on your space!" she apologibed, but Lloyd, missing the sarcasm, just nodded and kept reading.

BLUNDERSCHEDULE

Blunderschedule (v.) *'blun-dur-sked-jul* To incorrectly record the date and time of an appointment, resulting in a social or professional snafu.

"Oh no! Our Sufjan tickets were for last night, not tonight! I totally blunderscheduled."

CANCELLELATION

Cancellelation (**n.**) *'kan-sul-ee-'lay-shun* The joy felt by someone who frees up his schedule by canceling an appointment or reneging on a social plan.

Davina knew she ought to feel guilty for bailing on Mariel's dinner at the last minute, but a delicious cancellelation surged through her as Clive brought out the Scrabble board.

CANONBAIL

Canonbail (v.) *'kan-nun-bayl* To intend to spend one's leisure hours reading great works of literature, only to end up choosing less lofty fare.

Nina packed Moby-Dick *for the train ride to East Hampton, but at Penn Station she canonbailed and bought a handful of trashy magazines from a newsstand.*

CINAMNESIA

Cinamnesia (**n.**) *sin-nam-'nee-zha* The common condition of forgetting or misremembering scenes, actors, plot points, or dialogue in movies you think you know by heart (a condition whose sufferers often fail to realize their affliction).

> *Bruno's cinamnesia made his team lose the quiz bowl, when he insisted it was Tippi Hedren, not Kim Novak, who starred in* Vertigo.

DELIBEROT

Deliberot **(v.)** *duh-'lib-ur-rot* To waste hours, days, or years mulling over a situation until it's too late to amend it.

Should she give up acting and become a therapist? Nadia deliberotted for a decade, never getting around to applying to grad school, and never getting a part in a show that lasted longer than a few weeks.

ENVY-PREEMPT

Envy-preempt (**v.**) *'en-vee-pree-empt* To play down or deny your good fortune in the (usually) vain and (always) transparent hope that this might keep people from resenting you.

Cyril drove Walter nuts with his constant complaints about the heating bills in his huge house and his Jaguar's frequent breakdowns. Walter knew Cyril was envy-preempting and wished he would indulge in some honest gloating for a change.

FAKEWAKE

Fakewake (**n.**) *'feyk-weyk* The condition of being technically awake, but mentally still sleep-clouded.

Tom set his alarm for six, but lolled around in fakewake for hours after it went off, muzzily reading Gmail on his phone before getting out of bed around nine.

PARAHALING

Parahaling (**v.**) *'payr-a-hay-ling* Things cigarette smokers do to replace the addictive aspects of smoking when they quit, like chewing Nicorette when they feel a craving, or compulsively updating their Facebook status.

Amanda hated the gnawed-on toothpicks and gobbets of chewing gum that had started popping up around the house since Carter quit smoking, but figured the mess created by his parahaling was worth putting up with if it meant he stayed quit.

PHRASEFREEZE

Phrasefreeze (**v.**) *'frayz-freez* To forget what you meant to say, or to find yourself unable to make a retort even though it's on the tip of your tongue. Also (**adj.**) **Phrasefrozen**

After commandeering the attention of the table for eight minutes with an endless shaggy-dog joke, Oliver phrasefroze, unable to remember the punch line.

RATIONALOSER

Rationaloser (**n.**) *'ra-shun-a-'loo-zur* One who not only will tolerate a disagreeable status quo, but will convince herself that it's excellent—anything rather than contemplate change of any sort. Also (**v.**) **Rationalose** (q.v. **Deliberot**)

Why hadn't Darya quit her job, since her boss had told her he would never promote her? Being a rationaloser, she told herself she was lucky to have a job at such a wonderful company, and that it would be stressful to be a manager anyway.

SHELF-THWARTED

Shelf-thwarted (**adj.**) *'shelf-'thwor-ted* Bewildered by the array of products on store shelves to the point that you can't make a choice, or that you buy things you didn't mean to.

Tad was so shelf-thwarted by the display of shiny shapes and colors lining the grocery aisles that he forgot what he'd come to buy.

SIDEGAZE

Sidegaze (v.) *'syd-gayz* To obliquely watch something or someone, or to surreptitiously peek at what someone else is reading.

Everyone on the subway car was either playing Sudoku on their Kindles, or sidegazing at someone else's screen.

UNDERSHRUNK

Undershrunk (**adj.**) *un-dur-'shrunk* Describing high-strung souls who have chosen not to seek psychotherapy, but who could use it.

> *"Guys, I'm fine!" Stefan shrieked at his brunch companions. "I'm just stressed. I've got a lot on my plate, and I wish you'd quit dropping the names of your shrinks!"*
>
> *"But Stefan," said Vanessa. "You are so undershrunk. Seriously, let me give you Dr. Marshko's number."*

WILLPOWER OUTAGE

Willpower outage (**n. phrase**) *'wil-pow-er 'ow-tudj* The moment when, after days, weeks, even months of heroic self-discipline (dieting, exercising, quitting smoking) you crumble.

"Don't do it!" Sean implored, as Ursula slid from their booth at the diner, bent on buying a pack of cigarettes from the bodega across the street. "This is just a willpower outage, you haven't smoked for almost a year!"

"We're on vacation," Ursula retorted, and walked out the door.

VI.

Wired World

If your great-great-grandparents were teleported to the present, they would think they'd landed in a science-fiction movie and cover their eyes. The digital era that arrived late in the last century turned human beings into walking, talking telephone poles, complete with dangling, tangling wires. Screens replaced eye contact, instantaneous electronic communication could be achieved with the tap of a button; and suddenly, nobody, anywhere, could hide from bosses, relatives, or stalkers; a flashing screen and insistent ping could track anyone down, even on a beach in Ibiza. Ahh, the miracle of progress . . .

BINARY CONFINEMENT

Binary confinement (**n. phrase**) *'by-nuh-ree kun-'fyn-ment*
The self-imposed social isolation of excessively wired people.

Derek's roommate tried to persuade him to go to parties every weekend, but Derek preferred to sit alone at his computer, surfing the net, playing online games, and Gchatting, wallowing in binary confinement.

CELL-MELL

Cell-mell (**adv.**) *'sell-'mell* The reckless, life-threatening manner in which people text or talk on their cell phones while driving, bike riding, or walking in traffic.

Walking cell-mell across the intersection, Andy was so absorbed in texting his girlfriend that he nearly got hit by a truck, and didn't even look up from his BlackBerry when the brakes squealed.

CHARITEXT

Charitext (**n.**) *'chayr-i-tekst* A suddenly ubiquitous form of charitable donation, made impulsively via text message, and charged to the sender's phone bill.

After getting a phone bill for $300, tender-hearted Maggie learned to keep her cell phone out of reach when she watched the news, because whenever a tornado bashed a town or some other tragedy struck, she couldn't help charitexting.

DROIDIAN SLIP

Droidian slip (**n. phrase**) *'droy-dee-an slip* The contemporary predicament of confusing which electronic device does what; leading you to, for example, answer the AC remote instead of the cell phone, or to try to turn off the TV with the garage-door clicker.

> *Marina pulled her finger across the image to enlarge it, got mad when it stayed small, then realized she'd made a droidian slip—she was reading a regular magazine, not a tablet.*

EARDUDS

Earduds (**n. pl.**) *'eer-duds* Those who appear in public with headphones or earbuds clamped to their heads, tuning out everyone around them, and/or addressing invisible interlocutors.

> *Millennium Park was definitely cool, Rafa thought. He loved public sculpture. But all the expressionless earduds walking around the Bean weirded him out. They made the place look like it had been invaded by cyborgs, and made him miss Parc Güell back home in Barcelona.*

ESERVATIONS

Eservations (**n. pl.**) *'ee-zur-'vay-shunz* Reservations made online. Also (**v.**) **Eserve**

> *Mrs. Liu showed up for the Chinatown bus an hour early, planning to buy a ticket on board, but when she got there she found out that the seats were fully eserved, and she should have made an eservation several days ahead.*

ETITEXT

Etitext (**n.**) *'et-i-'tekst* Social behavior (often bad) connected with the use of cell phones and PDAs.

> *Kristina was shocked to see Danny Johnson typing on his phone throughout their teacher's funeral. What horrible etitext! If Mr. Dunne had been alive, he would have confiscated Danny's cell.*

FACEBOAST

Faceboast (**v.**) *'fayss-bohst* To use Facebook to trumpet your own triumphs.

Deirdre liked Mallory, and was relieved when she finally found a job. But after Mallory began incessantly Faceboasting about how gorgeous her new office was, how much praise she was getting, and even how magnificent her benefits were, Deirdre unfollowed her updates.

FACEBOOK-HAPPY

Facebook-happy (**adj. phrase**) *'fayss-book-'hap-pee* Describing one who attempts to convey exaggerated joie de vivre through artificially upbeat Facebook posts. Like "Broadway hot," it's a phrase that diminishes the strength of the adjective in question (i.e., not-so-very hot; not-so-very happy).

Ben was depressed when his ex posted photos of herself on Facebook looking ecstatic with a new guy. "I don't buy it," his friend Ali said. "I bet she's just Facebook-happy. The guy in the picture is probably her waiter at Chili's."

FAUXF

Fauxf (**v.**) *'fofe* Past tense: fauxfed *'fofed* To add strangers or distant acquaintances to your Facebook friends list, although they have no reason to communicate with you. A homonym for the acronym FOAFF—Friend of a Facebook Friend. (Also may be used as noun, denoting a non-actual friend on your Friend list.)

After going to her high school reunion, Sheila was fauxfed by three guys she barely remembered before she stopped answering friend requests.

MACALOON

Macaloon (**n.**) *'mack-a-loon* One who is loyal to Macintosh computers to the point of obsession.

> *Rob got his first Mac, a Classic, back in the early nineties. Twenty years and five Macs later, he was a proud Macaloon. He felt pity and a little distaste for the benighted souls who used PCs.*

OLDLINERS

Oldliners (**n. pl.**) *'old-'ly-nurz* Those who stubbornly cling to old-fashioned landline phones.

> *"Mom, you're such an oldliner. Why don't you have a cell phone?" Candace teased.*
>
> *"Don't be silly," her mother said. "Cell phones probably cause cancer, and besides, what if there's a power outage someday?"*

OSMUSIS

Osmusis (n.) *oz-'myoo-sis* The process by which you absorb someone else's musical tastes, willy-nilly, as the songs they're listening to leak from their headphones, earbuds, or streaming radio, or pop up among your AirPlay playlists.

"Great band," Forrest said to Jono. "How'd you find out about them?"

"Through osmusis," Jono said. "Heard them through the wall, from the guy next door's Pandora."

PHONEDEAF

Phonedeaf (adj.) *'fone-def* A (feigned) inability to recognize one's own phone's ringtone. A condition that commonly kicks in when the phone rings in an awkward setting.

"Are you phonedeaf?" Amanda hissed to the man next to her at the opera, whose phone shrilled throughout "Un Bel Di."

"Oh . . . was that my *phone?" he whispered innocently, reaching down to put the cell on silent.*

PHOTOFLOP

Photoflop (v.) *'fo-to-flop* To take photographs but forget to download them for so long that you forget what they were and erase them, or lose them altogether when the device you took them on is lost, broken, or stolen.

Cynthia and Greg took hundreds of pictures on their honeymoon, but photoflopped when they got home. On their first anniversary, they went to download the pictures, and found out they'd thrown away the memory cards.

ROBORAGE

Roborage (**n.**) *'ro-bo-raydzh* The anger that overtakes you after a succession of robocalls or telemarketing calls.

> *"What do you want now?" Harry shouted into the phone, when it rang for the fourth time in five minutes. "Oh, sorry, Mom," he mumbled. "That was just roborage. I just got three calls in a row from telemarketers."*

SCREENSTRESSED

Screenstressed (**adj.**) *'skreen-strest* To be bleary, red-eyed, and weary from spending too many consecutive hours staring at a computer screen.

Right after work, Marly had to rush to a gala dinner. She turned off her computer and went to the ladies' room to change and refresh her makeup, but she couldn't hide her glazed, screenstressed eyes.

SPAMBUSH

Spambush (**v.**) *'spam-bush* To barrage the e-mail inbox of an unwitting person with undesired sales pitches, newsletters, and fundraising appeals after mining their data online. Also (**n.**) the act of conducting such a barrage.

After taking an I.Q. test that popped up on a website he was reading, Alex was spambushed by online hucksters. With an I.Q. of 143, he should have known better than to click on the pop-up box.

TAGARAZZI

Tagarazzi (**n. pl.**) *'tag-gur-'otz-ee* Those who post pictures of friends and relatives on the Web without consulting them, tagging them for all to see.

Every time he went on Facebook, Ward would spend an hour tracking down party photos his tagarazzi friends had posted, and pleading with them to take them down before his teetotaler parents got wind of them.

T.M.I.M

T.M.I.M (**acronym**) *(Too-Much-I.M.-ing)* The common pastime of wasting hours, days, weeks unproductively instant-messaging.

Clark spent most of his time at the office at his keyboard, furiously typing. He assumed his colleagues thought he was working, but in fact he was nearly always I.M.ing on Gchat. When he got fired, he was stunned. "T.M.I.M.," his boss explained. "You were hired to do a job, not to instant-message your brother all day long."

UNISPAMMER

Unispammer (**n.**) *'yoo-nih-spam-mur* Friend or family member who bombards everyone's inbox with canned gags, article links, and the like.

As soon as Rory's name popped up in her inbox, Margaret hit delete, knowing that Rory was an incurable unispammer, and there'd be nothing in his e-mail but the newest batch of crude Wall Street jokes, plus maybe some LOL-cats.

VII.

Romance

How can you know if he really loves you—particularly when he spends intimate dinners gazing obsessively into his Black-Berry screen; and how can you be sure she's telling the truth if she says she didn't answer your call because she was on the other line? Was she? Or was she Gchatting with a stranger? Also, by the way, is there a sure way to tell if the object of your fascination is straight or gay? Or—as Daphne said to Osgood—might you be barking up the wrong fish? Never have the lovestruck faced more perplexing times, as the borders of socially sanctioned love, courtship, and marriage have melted and broadened, allowing competition to materialize out of thin air. And yet, happily, true love endures for the fortunate few, giving everyone else the courage to persevere. Well, mostly.

ANHEL

Anhel (**n.**) *'ahn-hell* Derived from the Spanish pronunciation of *angel* and the medical condition of anhedonia (to take no pleasure in pleasurable activities), an anhel is a man or woman who has no sex drive.

> *When Jared made no moves after a couple months of dating, Emma complained to friends that she'd made the mistake of falling for an anhel. Actually, though, he was just on Prozac.*

ASTAIRE

Astaire (**n.**) *uh-'stare* A man who people assume (or insist) is gay, even if he dates women, and even if he's married and has children—often because he's attractive, well dressed, polite, and good at dancing or singing.

> *Hugo had a wife, three kids, and a Rottweiler. Ever since he'd tap danced at an office party, his colleagues had gossiped that he was gay, but he wasn't: Hugo was a textbook astaire.*

BOBCAT

Bobcat (**n.**) *'bob-kat* Young man who desires and pursues older women, though he may also date younger women, and probably does. Far more prevalent than that other mythologized feline, the "cougar"—an older woman who seeks out younger men.

"Let's go see Chéri," *said Juliet.*

"That movie about the Parisian cougar and the young dude?" asked Robert.

"Please," Juliet harrumphed. "That guy is a bobcat, he chases her!"

CAFOODLING

Cafoodling (**n.**) *ka-'foo-duh-ling* Common activity of lovey-dovey couples who feed each other in public. Also (**v.**) **Cafoodle**

Walter and Ben had met for a business lunch, but were so distracted by the cafoodling couple at the table next to theirs, amorously slipping oysters into each other's mouths, that they asked the waiter to move them to another table.

COOPLE

Coople (n.) 'koo-pul Inseparable couple so satisfied by each other's company that they rarely socialize with others and seldom leave home.

"Don't invite Pauline and Kent on the rafting trip," Sarah said sadly. "They're such a coople now, there's no way they'll come, even if they say they will."

CREEPACEOUS PERIOD

Creepaceous period **(n. phrase)** *kree-'pay-shuss 'peer-ee-ud* The stage in the prehistory of a romance when you dissect your prospective partner's shortcomings with friends in gruesome detail.

Michael hoped none of the groomsmen at the rehearsal dinner would mention the awful things he'd said about Christabel back in the creepaceous period of their relationship, but his best man, predictably, dredged up the worst of them in his speech.

HATECRASHER

Hatecrasher (**n.**) *'hayt-krash-ur* An uninvited guest whose presence upsets or annoys hosts or other guests; particularly one who was expressly not invited but came anyway. Also (**v.**) **Hatecrash**

> *Dinah's back stiffened as Neil walked through the door, hatecrashing the party.* How dare he! *she thought. He'd broken up with Rose by text two weeks ago, and Dinah had promised her he wouldn't be there.*

KITTONITE

Kittonite (**n.**) *'kit-tun-nyt* The sapping, debilitating force that kittens and cats exert on a relationship when one of the partners despises all creatures of the feline persuasion.

"You and Rob broke up? What happened?"

"Well," said Harry, "remember my Burmese cat—Titus?"

"Of course."

"Titus was kittonite to us," he said somberly. "A month after Rob moved in, he admitted he hated cats and said either Titus would have to go or he would, so . . ."

MISSKISS

Misskiss (**n.**) *'mis-'kis* Unlike an air kiss, a misskiss is supposed to land on the cheek or lips, but misses its mark.

As Samantha rushed out the door to work, she spun around to kiss John good-bye, but he turned the wrong way and she ended up giving him a misskiss, her mouth engulfing his nose.

PALIMPSEX

Palimpsex (**n.**) *'pal-ump-seks* Indiscriminate flings conducted after a breakup to overlay memories of the departed.

After he and Gillian split up, Fred sent her mountains of flowers and sheaves of poignant notes for months, while at the same time indulging in epic palimpsex with every willing woman he met.

PLACEBEAU

Placebeau (**n.**) *pluh-see-'boh* A presentable, sociable man, gay or straight, who enjoys attending formal events with female friends, no strings attached.

> *Katia took her favorite placebeau to the opera instead of her new boyfriend, Nicolas, because she was afraid Nicolas would think she was too into him if she invited him to something so fancy in the first weeks of their relationship.*

POIVROTTE

Poivrotte **(n.)** *pwah-'vrut* French for a "female rummy" or boozer—that is, a woman who drinks more than she should. (More literal translation: pepperhead. An expression ripe for American import.)

It was two a.m. at SkyBar, and the poivrottes were in full force, slipping a little on their barstool perches, talking more loudly than they realized, and still slurping their spilling saketinis.

POLTERGUY

Polterguy (**n.**) *'pol-tur-gī* Ex-boyfriend who exerts a haunting, destructive influence on a person's later relationships.

Augusta had just gotten engaged to Sam when her polterguy, Mitchell, called out of nowhere, and told her he was coming to town and had to see her.

PROCRASTIDATE

Procrastidate (**v.**) ***pro-'kras-ti-dayt*** 1) To put off dating for a variety of reasons (workaholism, intimacy issues, addiction to *World of Warcraft*). 2) To date unseriously to avoid a genuine attachment.

> *After his divorce, Eric went through the motions of dating, but because he was really just procrastidating, he would break up with each girlfriend after a few months, so the question of marriage would never come up.*

SMOOVE

Smoove **(n.)** *'smoov* A man who, like the author of the satirical "Smoove B" column in the *Onion*, uses heavy-handed courtship methods that repel his target.

As Donovan, hair-gelled and American Appareled from head to toe, sidled up to a group of women at Radegast in a cloud of cologne, the women rolled their eyes and moved to the other side of the bar. "What a smoove," Courtney scoffed.

VELCRO ON

Velcro on (**phrasal v.**) *'vel-kro 'awn* To become genuinely enmeshed and attached in a romantic relationship. (Far less common than the reverse phenomenon: the failure to velcro on.)

"How are things with James?"

"Oh, fairly pointless. We're having fun, but he's not really velcroing on—there's no real lasting connection, so I'm losing interest."

VIII.

Fasting, Feasting, and Carousing

Back in the days of *Mad Men* and *Downton Abbey*, the crown of the social calendar was the dinner party, and witty conversation was its jewel. But today's hosts and hostesses are mostly too hyperscheduled to orchestrate elaborate feasts, and their equally busy guests prefer informal get-togethers—and have a constellation of issues about food. If you plan a dinner in the twenty-first century, you must first find out what your guests don't eat, then accept the fact that they're unlikely to show up on time—if they even remember to RSVP. Once assembled, both fasters and feasters mingle amiably enough with one another and their handheld electronic devices. Conversation may not sparkle; but how will you meet anybody if you don't budge from your sofa?

ANOCLEANSIC

Anocleansic (**n.**) *an-no-'klenz-ik* One who regularly engages in faddish liquid starvation diets known as cleanses. Also (**n.**) **Anocleansia,** the name of this compulsion.

> *When she was on her own, Lily consumed little but green juice, but when she was out with friends, she would order pizza and rich desserts so nobody would suspect her anocleansia.*

BLOTTER

Blotter **(n.)** *'blah-tur* Food eaten during (or after) a night of revelry to soak up alcohol and stave off (or soothe) a hang-over. Also **(pl.) Blotters**

Dave threw Ilya's stag party at a Brighton Beach club because he knew that even though there'd be vats of vodka, there'd also be lots of heavy food to sop it all up, and those blotters would keep the groomsmen from ending up in the hospital.

CANAPIG

Canapig (**n.**) *'kan-nuh-pig* Guest at a cocktail gathering who stuffs his (or her) face with hors d'oeuvres, making a meal out of canapés that were meant to feed a throng. (A *canapig* is by definition someone who **overdoeuvres** [q.v.].)

> *"That man is such a canapig! He ate the entire tray of chicken satay skewers while we were chatting."*

CLUSTERFÊTE

Clusterfête (n.) *'klus-tur-'fet* A day (or night) on which multiple events are scheduled, making it challenging (or impossible) to attend them all.

Clementine was frustrated that so much was going on tonight. One friend had a play opening, another had a birthday dinner, there was a Punch Brothers concert, plus two rooftop barbecues. What a clusterfête!

CROCKHEAD

Crockhead (**n.**) *'krok-hed* One who wholeheartedly and obsessively orchestrates meal preparation at family gatherings and share houses.

> *"Go ahead to the beach without me, I've got to stuff four dozen mushrooms for tapas."*
> *"Don't be a crockhead, Tabitha—it's only eleven a.m.!"*

FACTOSE INTOLERANT

Factose intolerant (**adj. phrase**) *'fak-tose in-'tall-er-unt* To shun certain foods out of the belief (based on no medical evidence) that you have acquired a severe allergy to them.

Verena wanted to throw a dinner party, but couldn't, because so many of her friends were factose intolerant. In recent months, because of whatever they'd been reading, Jerry and Max had decided they couldn't eat wheat, Jen was now "allergic" to dairy, and Margita and Lori would not eat fish (mercury) or red meat. What was left to serve?

MEALBREAKER

Mealbreaker (**n.**) *'meel-bray-kur* One who drains cheer from a group meal by not partaking of the food, or (if at a restaurant) by ordering a tiny appetizer and seceding from the group bill.

Why a woman who consumed nothing but kale and Pellegrino would want to belong to a gourmet club was a mystery to Carmen. She would never have invited Dana to join hers if she'd known she was a mealbreaker.

MEEHEE

Meehee (**n.**) *'me-he* Person who laughs at his own jokes and anecdotes. Also (**v.**) to laugh at one's own jokes and anecdotes.

> *Milton cracked up so hard telling the story of their jet-skiing mishap that his wife had to intervene to finish it so everyone would get the joke—knowing that, by this point, her meehee husband was too overcome with hilarity to be coherent.*

NAMEDREDGE

Namedredge (**v.**) *'naym-dredzh* At a social gathering, to desperately cue others to say aloud the name of a person in your midst whose name you have, to your shame, forgotten.

As Sage chatted with Katie, Violet, and a woman whose name escaped her, she spent ten minutes namedredging in vain. None of her friends produced the mystery woman's name.

NARCOFESTER

Narcofester (**n.**) *'nar-ko-fes-tur* A person who is prone to falling asleep at parties. Also (**n.**) **Narcofesty,** the condition suffered by narcofesters.

As Giselle and Renata laughed madly in a corner of the crowded room, they noticed Norman slumped on a sofa, dead asleep, mouth open, snoring. He had, once again, succumbed to narcofesty.

NOSOH

NOSOH (**acronym**) *'no-so* Unlike the GSOH—the person with a Good Sense of Humor so avidly sought in personal ads—the NOSOH has absolutely No Sense of Humor, gets no jokes, and is about as valuable at a social gathering as a no-show (perhaps less).

> *As Felix told them about his spree in Mongolia that ended (briefly) in a yurt jail, everyone doubled over laughing except for Aurora, the group's NOSOH, who blurted that she didn't see the fun in criminal behavior.*

ORTATE

Ortate (**v.**) *'or-tayt* 1) To talk with your mouth full. 2) To speak, unaware that a scrap of food (*ort* in crossword puzzle parlance) is stuck to your teeth or face.

Lavinia couldn't register what Dwight was saying while he orated, a piece of fettuccine dangling from his lip.

OVERDOEUVRE

Overdoeuvre (v.) *'o-vur-'durv* To eat so many appetizers that you lose your appetite for a meal. [q.v. ***Canapig***]

Victor pigged out on sushi and cashews at the art open-ing, and only realized as he left that he'd overdoeuvred, and would be too full to enjoy his long-awaited dinner at Gramercy Tavern with Dulcie.

R.B.S.

R.B.S. **(acronym)** *(Rather Be Sleeping) arr-bee-ess'* A classification pertaining to entertainments so tedious, unsatisfying, or off-putting that anyone watching or participating in them would Rather Be Sleeping.

"How was the symphony?"

"Strictly R.B.S. I know everyone loves Debussy, but I couldn't keep my eyes open. I actually fell asleep in the second half."

RECIPLAY

Reciplay (**v.**) *'ress-i-play* To cook without a recipe, adding a little bit of this, a little bit of that, sometimes producing a triumph, sometimes a mess.

Ethan prided himself on his freestyle way of cooking without recipes, cookbooks, or measuring spoons—even when the results of his reciplaying were inedible.

SLIPSOCKED

Slipsocked **(adj.)** *'slip-sokt* To be caught wearing dingy, tattered, or mismatched socks at a gathering where hosts make guests take off their shoes before entering.

Jackson had hoped to meet somebody new at Elaine's brunch. But she made everyone leave their shoes in the hall, so he walked around slipsocked, only talking to people he already knew, because he felt so self-conscious about his grubby socks, which had a hole in one toe.

SUROTRASH

Surotrash (**n.**) *'sur-ro-trash* Flashy, flirtatious, ultrasocial people from regions south (*sur*, in Spanish) of the United States—the Latin American variant of the Continental species known teasingly as Eurotrash. Also (**adj.**)

By day, Conor was an uptight investment banker, but on the weekend he liked to let loose at surotrash dance clubs where Spanish pop played, women dressed provocatively, men wore cologne and unbuttoned shirts, and everyone danced close.

UNDERTAIN

Undertain (v.) **un-dur-'tayn** 1) To give low-key parties that offer no special food, drink, or décor. 2) To host fewer social events than you ought to.

Stu and his friends hung out at each other's places a lot, and undertained the same way they had in college. Someone brought chips, someone brought beer, and someone would go to the deli to get more, as needed.

WINDOWALL

Windowall (**n.**) *'win-da-waul* An enclosed café or restaurant that feels alfresco because it has a wall of windows that opens up, letting in natural light and facilitating scoping between diners and flâneurs.

"Let's go to an outdoor café!" Sara suggested.
"Can we go to a windowall instead?" Gilbert asked. "It's just as summery, and we won't have to eat next to trash cans and honking taxis."

ZAGATTITUDE

Zagattitude (**n.**) *za-'gat-i-tood* Mindset of one who always has a firm, vocal opinion on where, what, and how to eat—informed by Zagat, Chowhound, and other foodie bibles.

They all just wanted pizza, but Blake, flexing his Zagattitude, insisted they go to a pricey new banh mi place he'd read about.

IX.

Domestic Life

Home, of late, is a place where one spends less time than one would wish. It is where the children are—if you have children—and the pets, bicycles, TiVo, and takeout menus. It is also where—with or without the presence of such moss—today's grown-ups recharge after a long day at work and, perhaps, the gym. Before the modern child is able to type or walk, much is done (sometimes too much) on the home front to keep him healthy, happy, and entertained, so he'll grow up as quickly as possible to be a well-adjusted, high-functioning member of our fast-paced society—just like you.

BABY-EINSTONED

Baby-einstoned (**adj. phrase**) *bay-bee-'ine-stoand* To be benumbed by a child's incessantly looping music, cartoon, and movie DVDs.

As Martin, carrying the suitcases, opened the door of their hotel room, followed by Corinna, carrying their son Gideon, the boy started wailing for his Baby Einstein DVD. No, Martin thought, *even on vacation there was no escape from being baby-einstoned.* As the Vivaldi and puppets kicked in, the crying stopped.

BABYSPLITTER

Babysplitter (**n.**) *'bay-bee-'split-tur* Childminder who cancels with little or no notice, on unsatisfactory pretexts.

For the third time that month, Ida called last-minute to tell Sarah and Dan she couldn't watch the kids that day. Sick of being at the mercy of their babysplitter's whims, Sarah told her she was fired, then called emergency day care.

BUGABOUND

Bugabound (**adj.**) *'bug-gah-bound* Encumbered by a bulky stroller and the child within it.

As Jared pushed Tallulah down the crowded sidewalk in her stroller, he noticed a tiny café. He longed to duck in and get an éclair, but there was no way to maneuver the wide buggy through the narrow door, and no room inside, anyway—he was bugabound.

DAWGLE

Dawgle (**v.**) *'dog-gul* To daydream about the joys of dog ownership and profess an overpowering love of dogs, but to take no steps that would actually bring one into your home.

Ed was determined to own a harrier dog one day, and had come up with the notional puppy's name a decade ago: Brutus. But he was just dawgling, and Ed's friends knew that no "Brutus" would ever materialize.

DISTRACTINATOR

Distractinator (**n.**) *dis-'trak-tih-nay-tur* An audiovisual device that holds a child's attention long enough to permit a parent to perform routine tasks.

Justin was talking to an irate client on the phone when Auggie and Dane started shrieking and thwacking each other with foam light sabers. Instinctively, Justin pressed Play on the DVD player. As Kung Fu Panda *came up on the distractinator, the boys put down their sabers.*

EXCHILLARATED

Exchillarated (**adj.**) *ex-'chil-lur-ayt-ud* Filled with exuberant, playful joy by cold, wintry weather. Also (**n.**) **Exchillaration**

Nat and Guinevere, their mittens encrusted with snow, took turns sledding down the hill, red-cheeked and laughing, exchillarated by the winter wonderland.

FELINE ALARM CLOCK

Feline alarm clock (**n.**) *'fee-lyn uh-'larm klok* Cat that wakes its owner in search of attention or food. (Counterpart to canine alarm clock, the dog version.)

Dylan set his Kindle to chime at seven-thirty p.m. instead of a.m. by mistake, but the feline alarm clock saved him at seven a.m., when Mittens leapt on his pillow.

FELONG

Felong (**v.**) *fee-'long* Of cats: to make a yearning, clutching noise in the throat while staring at birds they cannot catch.

> *Puff and Boots huddled on the windowsill for half an hour, felonging in frustration as they watched pigeons alight and depart unscathed.*

FERTILITOTS

Fertilitots (**n. pl.**) *fur-'til-lih-tots* Babies, often twins and trip-lets, conceived in fertility labs—a phenomenon occurring ever more frequently as couples delay childbearing.

Judging from the crush of dual and triple strollers at the playground, there was an epidemic of fertilitots in Blithe and Aaron's neighborhood. This made sense, since so many of the other parents were in their forties, just like them. They had probably had IVF, too, Blithe figured.

HUMOMMIATED

Humommiated (adj.) *hyew-'mom-me-ay-tud* Describing the intense feeling of embarrassment a child suffers when his mother does something like sing, dance, kiss him in public, or lick a Kleenex to clean his face. Also (n.) Humommiation

Jacob was humommiated when his mother performed a folk dance, in costume, for his class. How could he ever show his face in the third grade again?

JOLLYROLL

Jollyroll (**v.**) *'djah-lee-role* To laugh so hard and so infectiously that you provoke laughter in others.

As one-year-old Theo jollyrolled, overcome with mirth by the funny faces his toddler sister was making, their father started laughing, too.

KIDDOFLAGE

Kiddoflage (n.) *'kid-doe-flazh* When an adult uses little kids or preteens as cover to do something childish but fun that he secretly wants to do himself.

Worried that his wife would think he was babyish if he confessed his longing to see Disney's Cinderella, *Clark watched it with their daughters Lucie and Willa as kiddoflage.*

KINDERSCARE

Kinderscare (**n.**) *'kin-dur-skayr* The admissions process a toddler or child endures to gain admission to a select nursery school or kindergarten. Also (**adj.**) **Kinderscared:** Afraid that one's child will not get into an exclusive preschool.

When Monique boasted that Aisling had gotten into Montessori, Gretchen didn't tell her that Calum had been spooked by the kinderscare, and hadn't made the cut.

LOTOTOMIZED

Lototomized (**adj.**) *la-'tot-ah-myzd* Describing the feelings of confusion suffered by adults distracted by yammering children who need them.

> *Dara and Phil were sure that, unlike their friends with kids, they wouldn't be lototomized by the arrival of their twins. But almost as soon as the girls were born, they found themselves quitting the gym, seeing less of their friends, and feeling scatty and exhausted at all times. Before a year was out, they had traded their loft for a ranch house in the burbs.*

PAWSY

Pawsy (**n.**) *'poz-zee* Condition displayed by dogs and cats when their paws tremble as they sleep, imagining themselves chasing squirrels or the like.

Deep in a dream of running, the golden retriever puppy twitched so madly with pawsy that she sleep-ran herself off the sofa, tumbled to the carpet, and awoke with a surprised yip.

ROTTER

Rotter (**n.**) *'rah-tur* The plastic drawer in a refrigerator where fresh vegetables are put away to keep "crisp," but where, hidden away, they typically decay until they become foul sludge.

> *"While you're rooting through the fridge, don't open the rotter! I stuck some mushrooms and zucchini in there like half a year ago. . . . I promise you, you do not want to open that drawer."*

SHAFTLING

Shaftling (n.) *'shaft-ling* A child in a not especially dysfunctional family who gets less nurturing than the others for obscure reasons.

Maddie's rowdy brothers got more attention from their parents than she did, she thought. But she didn't mind being the shaftling, because she was self-sufficient and had a lot of friends. Not that her parents seemed to notice.

SHLEPERD

Shleperd (n.) *'shlep-urd* 1) A vigorous soul who forces others to participate in exhaustingly long walks in the name of culture, nature, exercise, or economy (for instance, dodging cab fare). 2) One who drives children and others to their various schools, offices, playdates, and extracurricular activities. Also (v.)

Gordon woke his visiting relatives at eight a.m., marched them twenty blocks to Chinatown for dim sum, then shleperded them to Grand Central for a day trip to Cold Spring.

SPOONLEAD

Spoonlead (**v.**) *'spoon-leed* To open your mouth wide when feeding a baby, in an unconscious effort to coax the baby to do the same.

> *As Derek tried to spoonlead Matilda her pureed carrots, she kept her mouth firmly shut no matter how wide he opened his. When he finally ate a spoonful himself to prove its deliciousness, Matilda opened her mouth just long enough to laugh at him.*

STAYFREE STUMBLES

Stayfree stumbles (**n. phrase**) *'stay-free 'stum-bulz* Spate of clumsiness that besets women at times of hormonal imbalance.

Lena knocked a cone of wet coffee grounds off the counter, then hit her head on the cabinet door as she tried to stop the filter from falling. When she slammed the cupboard door, all the spice jars skittered off the under-shelf. This could mean only one thing, she realized: the Stayfree stumbles were upon her.

TYRANNITOT

Tyrannitot (**n.**) *ty-'ran-i-tot* Child who is permitted (or encouraged) to dominate adult social gatherings and indulge its whims in all particulars.

The food at the dinner was divine, but the guests had a wretched time, because the hosts let their tyrannitots rove freely, not even admonishing them when they clambered onto the dining table and walked barefoot among the plates.

WONDER DUTY

Wonder duty (**n. phrase**) *'wun-dur 'doo-tee* At holidays, the task of assembling presents, filling stockings, hiding Easter eggs or *afikomen*, etc., without being seen by the children. (A task that generally falls to the most guiltable adult.)

> *"God no, Mike—you can't make me do wonder duty! I've been up since dawn making Yule logs. If you don't assemble Trent's tricycle and Ashley's princess tent and put them by the tree, I'm leaving you."*

X.

In Transit

Progress means that hundreds of thousands of people commute every day to offices more than an hour from home; while jet travel means nobody thinks anything of flying a thousand miles (or more) for a brief vacation. But even if you walk to work or school or have a comparatively quick ride to work, you know that the perpetual motion of modern daily life is fraught with roadblocks and frustrations.

BAGGATORY

Baggatory (**n.**) *'bag-ga-to-ree* The limbo-like precincts of an airport baggage claim, where groggy travelers gather around the motionless treads of empty conveyor belts.

After a twelve-hour flight, Lowell spent several listless hours in baggatory at JFK, waiting with other passengers for their luggage to appear. Theirs came. His turned out to have ended up in Stockholm.

BERLITZKRIEG

Berlitzkrieg (**v.**) *bur-'lits-kreeg* A survival tactic adopted by travelers who use their linguistic cluelessness (pretended or real) to brazen their way through tricky situations in countries whose language they don't speak.

Arriving at Kabataş as the ferry was about to depart, Paula and John berlitzkrieged onto the boat without tickets, shouting, "Sorry, no speak Turkish!" as they hurtled through the turnstiles.

BUNGLEBAG

Bunglebag **(n.)** *'bun-gul-bag* Poorly packed piece of luggage.

Graham didn't start packing for his surfing vacation in South Africa until two hours before the flight, at which point he flung some clothes into a suitcase, hailed a taxi, and barely made it to the airport on time. He arrived in Durban with a bunglebag that held neither his wetsuit, his pajamas, nor his camera.

COACH CRUNCHERS

Coach crunchers (**n. pl.**) *'koach-krun-cherz* Frugal, hungry people who tote their own (rarely appetizing) meals onto airplanes.

> *The coach crunchers seated beside Maryam snacked noisily (and messily) on liverwurst sandwiches and hardboiled eggs throughout the flight.*

COMMUTIKAZE

Commutikaze (**v.**) *ka-'mew-ti-'kah-zee* To recklessly disregard traffic and safety hazards in the rush to get to or from work. Also (**n.**) one who commutikazes.

Luke commutikazed down the subway stairs, hoping to board the F train, and lunged unsuccessfully at the closing doors, getting his coat smeared with black grease in the process.

DAYTRAP

Daytrap (**n.**) *'dey-trap* A supposedly highly fun one-day outing that ends up being exhausting, expensive, and more trouble than it was worth.

On a crisp autumn Saturday, Dana and Skip drove four hours in traffic to go apple-picking. By the time they got there, the trees were picked bare, and they regretted their daytrap.

ELEVEXER

Elevexer (**n.**) *'el-uh-vek-sur* One who holds up the progress of an elevator by opening the closing doors at the last minute to squeeze in.

Karen was about to lose her mind. Not one, not two, but three elevexers held up the elevator on the way to the eighteenth floor, squeaking in with guilty smiles and false apologies as the doors were trying to close.

ESCAWAITER

Escawaiter (**n.**) *'es-ka-way-tur* Oblivious person who stands immobile on a moving staircase or walkway (often burdened with bags and baggage), blocking the progress of others.

Rushing up the escalator to make her flight, Emma was held up by a family of corpulent escawaiters who would not let her pass.

GP ASS

GP Ass **(n.)** *djee-pee-'ass* One who ignores common sense and blindly follows the instructions of the GPS, putting himself and passengers at risk of hurtling down mountainsides, driving into ditches, and so on.

> *"Look through the windshield, not at the Garmin!" Melanie shrieked as Dustin steered the rental car toward a drainage ditch. "You're such a GP ass! Can't you see this isn't a road?"*

LOCKBLOCK

Lockblock **(n.)** *'lok-blok* The state of confusion that assails you as you leave your house, in which you lock the door only to have to reopen it, as you remember something crucial you needed to do before you left. Also **(v.) Lockblocked**

Don lockblocked three times as he left his apartment for work, first because he'd forgotten his briefcase, next when he remembered he needed his tennis racket, and finally to turn off the iron.

MAX LEGROOM

Max Legroom (**n. phrase**) *'maks 'leg-room* Person on a train, bus, or airplane who reclines her seat fully, with total disregard for the comfort of the person behind her.

The selfish Max Legroom on the Acela Express kept his seat all the way back throughout the three-hour trip. Unable to open her own tray table, Lila kicked the seat-back from time to time.

NAGIVATOR

Nagivator (**n.**) *'nag-i-vay-tor* Passenger who continually questions the driver's handling of a car, second-guesses every turn, and criticizes speed, braking technique, signaling, etc. Also (**v.**) **Nagivate**

"YES, I see the exit, Erin, stop nagivating! That's why I got the GPS!"

NYET-SETTERS

Nyet-setters **(n. pl.)** *'nyet-set-turs* The flock of cash-flush New Russians who, since the midnineties, have been popping up in the world's choicest hot spots and finding fault with them. Also **(n.) Nyet-setting**

> *Patricia was sipping a frappé by the harbor in Khania when a limo unloaded a pack of Versace-clad nyet-setters, who gathered grumpily in front of her table, arguing in Russian, smoking, and blocking her view.*

PARKING SPACED

Parking spaced (v.) *'par-king 'spayst* To have forgotten where you parked your car, particularly in some sprawling, multi-tiered lot attached to a sports, shopping, or institutional complex.

> *When Kara left the mall after spending the afternoon back-to-school shopping, she completely parking spaced. It took her twenty minutes to figure out which lot she'd left the Subaru in.*

RAZORGEEZER

Razorgeezer (**n.**) *'ray-zur 'ghee-zur* Post-adolescent man or woman who zooms about town on a Razor or other foot-propelled scooter.

Emmeline stepped into the bike lane and nearly was run down by a man in his forties on a scooter, going the wrong way. He was the best-looking Razorgeezer she'd ever seen, but she shook her fist at him anyway.

SIDEBLOCKERS

Sideblockers (**n. pl.**) *'syd-blok-kurz* Pedestrians who walk aimlessly or slowly on sidewalks and public thoroughfares, usually accompanied by a cluster of similarly clueless pals. Also (**v.**) **Sideblock** and (**ger.**) **Sideblocking**

> *Amanda was trying to make the 5:45 train out of Penn Station, but so many sideblockers got in her way along Seventh Avenue that she missed it.*

SLURPWALKING

Slurpwalking (**n.**) *'slurp-wok-king* The American habit of walking while drinking something—whether it be juice from a box, coffee from a cup, water from a bottle, or soda from a can.

While slurpwalking to the office, reading the morning paper, Irina failed to notice that her bottle of carrot juice had leaked, spilling a vivid orange stain down her coat.

VELORAPTOR

Veloraptor (**n.**) *'veh-lo-rap-ter* Person hostile to bicyclists, who drives or walks in such a manner as to put cyclists at risk of injury or death.

Every time she rode her bike, Monique nearly got killed. Dodging potholes was hard enough—but it was the veloraptors swerving at her in taxis and pedestrians darting into the bike lane that were the real hazard.

XI.

Sports and Leisure

Given the ever-lengthening hours that everyone now spends sitting in a chair staring at a screen, leisure has taken on a distinctly unleisurely character of late—at least theoretically. Many members of our seated citizenry, fearing deep-vein thrombosis and calcification, or embarrassed by their sloth-like habits, bestir themselves in untethered moments to hop on treadmills, ride bikes, scale mountains, and attend (or even participate in) rowdy sporting events, whether out of actual inclination, or out of guilt. The impulse may be admirable, but results are mixed.

CHILLSEEKER

Chillseeker (**n.**) *'chil-see-kur* One who invites catarrh by exercising outdoors in sub-freezing temperatures, or by wearing light clothing in wintry weather.

The chillseekers jounced through the frigid park in thermal jog togs, dutifully running their miles before work as howling wind gusts sent snow sifting down from the pines.

DISADFANTAGED

Disadfantaged (**adj.**) *dis-ad-'fan-tudzhd* To be hindered professionally and socially by ignorance of (or lack of interest in) sports and spectatorship.

> *Tim hated basketball. Even so, when his colleagues didn't invite him to watch a March Madness game with them, it stung, and he resented being disadfantaged.*

EXERSKIVING

Exerskiving (**n.**) *'ek-ser-sky-ving* Dressing up in gym clothes, intending to work out, but not quite managing it. (Exerskiving can look like exercising but does little to boost the heart rate.) Derived from *exercise* + *skive* (Brit): to be lazy or to avoid work.

Claudia put on her yoga outfit and headed to the Bikram studio, but when she got outside, it was so cold that she exerskived instead, jog-walking to a pastry shop and getting a cocoa and a muffin.

EXHORTICISE

Exhorticise (v.) *eg-'zor-ti-syz* To trumpet the virtues of exercise, and urge others to do strenuous workouts—a common pastime of triathletes and other fitness obsessives.

After going on Atkins, losing two hundred pounds, and becoming an Ironman, Sebastian exhorticised his friends to become as healthy and athletic as he was.

ICYCLIST

Icyclist **(n.)** *'eye-sik-list* One who bicycles in winter, when streets are filled with snow and ice.

Despite the snowstorm, a few foolhardy icyclists were out on the street, skidding on the bike lanes flinging slush.

JAWGLING

Jawgling **(n.)** *'jawg-ling* Jogging while chatting with a friend, and moving so slowly that you're practically at a walk.

Petra and Ellie jawgled around the reservoir every Saturday morning, to the annoyance of the serious joggers who had to weave around them.

LOCKERGAWKER

Lockergawker (**n.**) '*lok-ker-gok-kur* Locker-room voyeur who sneaks peeks at others as they change clothes.

As she took off her swimsuit, Jill felt she was being watched. Quickly turning, she caught a lockergawker checking her out. The woman immediately whipped her head up, pretending she'd been looking at the wall clock.

LOCKTIMIST

Locktimist **(n.)** *'lok-ti-mist* A gymgoer who leaves work clothes, wallet/purse, laptop, or other valuables in an unlocked locker. Also **(adj.) Locktimistic** and **(n.) Locktimism**

"You're leaving your stuff in there unlocked? I used to be a locktimist, too—until someone stole my Uggs."

NAUTILUST

Nautilust (n.) *'not-i-lust* At a gym, the desire felt by one gym-goer for another, generally producing a creeped-out feeling in the ogled party. Also (v.)

As she jogged on the treadmill, Tizia felt persistent nautilust beaming from the guy next to her. After a few minutes, she fled to the weight room to avoid his gaze.

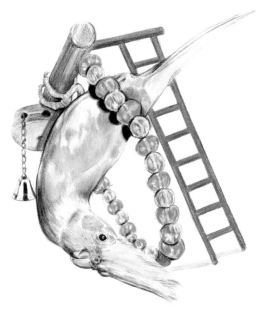

OBSTACYCLE

Obstacycle **(n.)** *'ob-sta-sy-kul* Bike (real or stationary) stored in a city apartment, where it takes up space, gets in the way, and is rarely ridden, as it's so inconvenient to move.

After Rich's bike was stolen off the street, he bought a new one and kept it at the foot of his bed. Almost immediately, it became nothing but an obstacycle that he tripped over every time he went to his sock drawer, and rarely carried downstairs.

PROSPLASHTINATION

Prosplashtination (**n.**) *pro-'splash-ti-'nay-shun* The act of postponing entry into a lake, river, sea, ocean, or swimming pool for fear that the water will be bone-chillingly cold. Also (**v.**) **Prosplashtinate**

Imogen, who'd grown up on the gelid coast of Wales, sprinted fearlessly into the surf on Memorial Day weekend. The others hung back, teeth chattering, suffused with prosplashtination.

SATURDAZED

Saturdazed (**adj.**) *'sat-er-dayzd* The way one feels after spending a lazy Saturday sleeping in, watching reruns on a tablet in bed, Facebooking, and napping.

Corinna got back from the charity 5k run to find Larry saturdazed, lying groggily in bed, an empty pint of Häagen-Dazs on the floor beside him. When she scolded him for his torpor, he mustered the energy for a twilight walk.

SNOW-MO

Snow-mo (**n.**) *'sno-mo* The sluggish, hampered movement of people who try to walk in heavy slush and snow while thickly clad in parkas and boots. Also, in longer form, **Snow-motion**

They couldn't hail a taxi in the blizzard, so they ended up walking the twenty blocks home, skittering on ice patches and clambering over frozen drifts in awkward snow-mo.

VACOMACATION

Vacomacation (**n.**) *vah-'ko-ma-'kay-shun* A holiday spent chiefly napping, avoiding boisterous or strenuous group activities.

While the others peeled off to bike to the lighthouse, play tennis, or climb the dunes, Lars installed himself on the sofa, where he dozed for six hours, a book propped over his face, reveling in his vacomacation.

VELOCIFEED

Velocifeed (**v.**) *'vuh-'loss-i-feed* To eat while you are on the move, whether on foot or on wheels.

Don tugged a PowerBar out of its wrapper while cycling across the bridge and ate it hungrily, nearly running down a jogger as he was velocifeeding.

XII.

The Money Pit

So, you've lost your job and your house, your 401(k) has melted to nothing, tuition payments are due, and the global economy continues to stagger. Why worry? Such economic hiccups will seem meaningless a hundred years from now . . . to somebody who is not you, does not know about your financial terrors, and is in no way connected to you. Then again, the long view is not particularly consoling to those of us who are engaged in the current scramble to achieve or restore solvency in a challenging job climate, as the stock market continues to jitter and carom like a greased pinball.

CELEBROKE

Celebroke (**adj.**) *'sel-a-broke* The miserable yet avoidable financial state of one who blows through a cash windfall before it arrives, or overspends upon receiving it.

Hilary was so giddy when she learned she was getting a tax refund that she bought a new couch, a dress, and a gym membership; at which point she was celebroke, with only three dollars to see her to her next paycheck.

DREAMODELING

Dreamodeling (**n.**) *dree-'mod-duh-ling* The wish-fulfilling visions your subconscious concocts while you sleep, in which you discover that your apartment or house has guestrooms, terraces, libraries, etc. that you somehow had failed to perceive in waking like. Also (**v.**) **Dreamodel**

Dorrie leapt out of bed eager to play a Bach étude on her piano. Seconds later, she realized she'd been dreamodeling . . . and her tiny studio did not have a kitchen table, much less the airy, sunlit room she'd conjured in her sleep.

GREENFLEECE

Greenfleece **(v.)** *'green-fleess* To charge exorbitant prices for organic and/or locally sourced products. Also **(adj.)** **Green-fleeced**

> *Lucas sped through Whole Foods scooping up an armload of artisanal cheeses, bread, olives, and organic crudités for a cocktail party. The bill came to $120. "Greenfleeced, again!" he groaned. Would he ever learn?*

HOUSEFLITTER

Houseflitter **(n.)** *'howss-flit-tur* Person who lives for months or years without a permanent address by jumping from one housesitting, catsitting, or plantsitting gig to the next. Also **(v.) Houseflit**

Although he hadn't sold a single screenplay during his five years in L.A., Avi lived comfortably because he was in such demand as a houseflitter. Soon after moving to town, he'd housesat for a celebrity, who spread the word that he was trustworthy and likable, and from then on, he'd never once had to pay rent.

MATTEROCRACY

Matterocracy (**n.**) *'Mat-tur-'ock-ra-see* The new power struc-
ture that has replaced the meritocracy, in which people gain
wealth and stature not through old-fashioned credentials
and tenacity, but by flexibly and shrewdly figuring out how to
make what they do *matter*. Also (**n.**) **Matterocrat** and (**adj.**)
Matterocratic

> *Kayla's Stanford degree and summa cum laude honors
> couldn't get her a job. But her younger brother, a nerdy
> MMOG freak, got rich at eighteen by making superhero
> mash-up videos that went viral. Unlike her, he came of
> age at the dawning of the matterocracy. Eventually he
> hired her to do PR for him.*

NEWPRESSION

Newpression **(n.)** *noo-'presh-un* The global economic crisis that began in 2007 as the housing market started collapsing, and lingered long thereafter.

> *Maureen had hoped to work for an investment bank after B-school, but because of the newpression, she ended up moving into her parents' basement and applying to the Peace Corps instead.*

PINSTRIPE PIRATES

Pinstripe pirates **(n. pl.)** *'pin-stryp 'py-rutz* Ruthless financiers who enrich themselves with bloated bonuses and inflated salaries, and use political clout to protect their power and wealth.

> *After the financial crisis sunk the global economy in 2008, greedy pinstripe pirates at bailed-out banks awarded themselves millions in unearned bonuses with taxpayer dollars.*

PORTPHOBIO

Portphobio (**n.**) ***port-'fo-bee-o*** An investment portfolio whose worth has declined so terribly that you are afraid to look at it.

Reluctantly checking her portphobio, Gwynn asked herself for the twentieth time why she'd bought so many shares of Facebook stock.

SCHADENFROLIC

Schadenfrolic (**n.**) *'shah-den-frah-lik* A party held in a spirit of commiseration, not celebration, to mark the extinction of a newspaper, magazine, blog, bank, restaurant, business, etc.; and/or the firing or laying off of an employee or employees.

"What are you taking to Bob's schadenfrolic?"
"He said beer, but I figured I'd bring a bottle of Black Label Jack. It's the least I can do, since there's no way he'll be able to afford his own until he finds a new job."

ACKNOWLEDGMENTS

Wordbirds, from the start, has been a labor of love and whimsy. I began it as a Tumblr in March 2009, posting my neologisms as a beguiling distraction from my journalistic deadlines. Thanks go to every word- and bird-lover who "got it" early on, who circulated my *Wordbirds* when I posted them on Tumblr, Facebook, and Twitter, and who sent me suggestions for words they wanted birdified.

Special gratitude goes to David Smith—for many years the "librarian to the stars" at the New York Public Library—who secured a spot for me at the library's Allen Room, where I wrote several score of the early entries; to Adam Wilson and Adam Baer, who brought *Wordbirds* to a wider audience on *The Faster Times* (www.thefastertimes.com); and to Stephanie Hodges, who devoted long hours to improving the Tumblr's look, sprucing up *Wordbirds'* plumage as we prepared to flutter it before publishers.

My heartfelt thanks go to my farseeing agent, Zoe Pagnamenta, who believed in *Wordbirds* from the time it was first fledged until it could soar; to my splendid editor at Simon & Schuster, Millicent Bennett, who made sure my definitions were as sharp and vivacious as possible; and to her amazingly helpful assistant, Sarah Nalle, who patiently and attentively wrangled the words and art as we brought them to paper. Thanks also to Dominick Anfuso of Free Press and to Jonathan Karp and Ben Loehnen of Simon & Schuster, whose enthusiasm helped ensure that *Wordbirds* would become a book.

Last but not least, my affectionate awe goes to the phenomenally talented and generous artist Elizabeth Zechel, who created the avian illustrations that help my coinages truly take flight.

—Liesl Schillinger
Paris, July 2013

ABOUT THE AUTHOR
AND THE ILLUSTRATOR

Liesl Schillinger is a journalist and translator based in New York. She is a regular contributor to the *New York Times Book Review,* a book columnist for the *New York Times Styles* section, and has written about literature, culture, theater, and travel for many publications, from the *New Yorker,* the *Washington Post*, and the *New Republic* to *Vogue* and the *Daily Beast.* Her Penguin Classics translation of *The Lady of the Camellias* by Alexandre Dumas (fils) came out in June 2013.

Elizabeth Zechel is an illustrator and author of the children's book *Is There a Mouse in the Baby's Room?* (Lark Books, a Division of Sterling Publishing Co., 2008). She has illustrated children's books such as *The Little General and the Giant Snowflake* by Matthea Harvey (Tin House Books, 2009) and cookbooks such as *Bubby's Homemade Pies* by Jen Bervin and Ron Silver (John Wiley & Sons, 2007) as well as a variety of magazines and literary journals. She lives and teaches kindergarten in Brooklyn.